D1436124

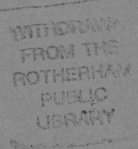

100% UNOFFICIAL FOOTBALL IDOLS

Your guide to England's
SENSATIONAL STRIKER:

KANE

DEAN

First published in Great Britain in 2021 by Dean,
part of Farshore.

An imprint of HarperCollins*Publishers*
1 London Bridge Street, London SE1 9GF
www.farshore.co.uk

HarperCollins*Publishers*
1st Floor, Watermarque Building, Ringsend Road
Dublin 4, Ireland

Written by Kevin Pettman
Edited by Craig Jelley
Designed by Grant Kempster and Jessica Coomber

This book is an original creation by Farshore

This unofficial guide is in no way connected to or sponsored by Harry Kane

100% Unofficial Football Idols: Kane © Farshore 2021

ISBN 978 0 7555 0204 2
Printed in Italy
1
A CIP catalogue record for this title is available from the British Library.

100% UNOFFICIAL

FOOTBALL IDOLS

Your guide to England's
SENSATIONAL STRIKER:

KANE

CONTENTS

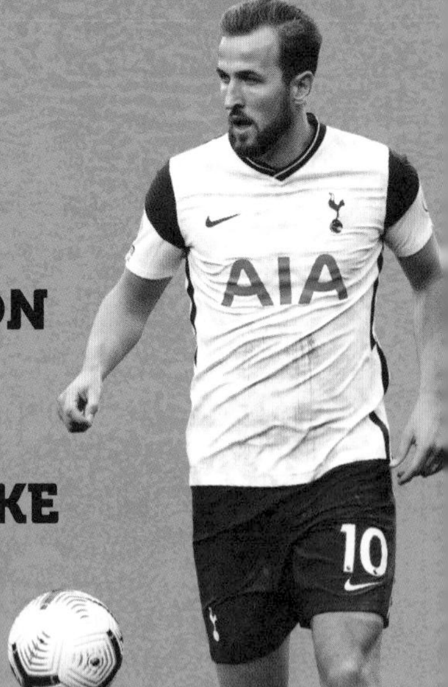

AIA
10

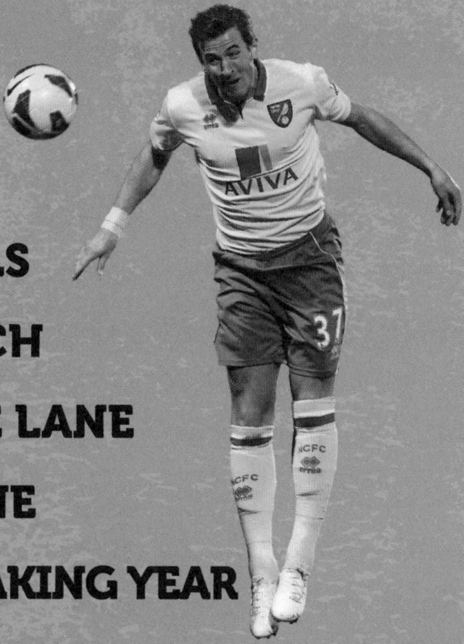
AVIVA

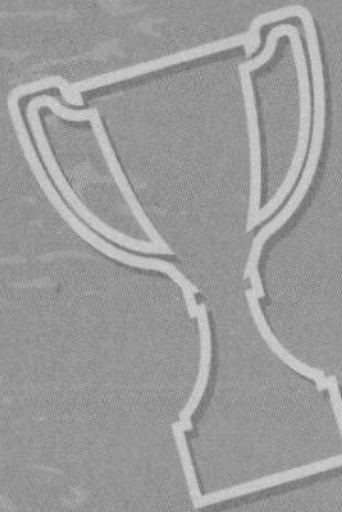

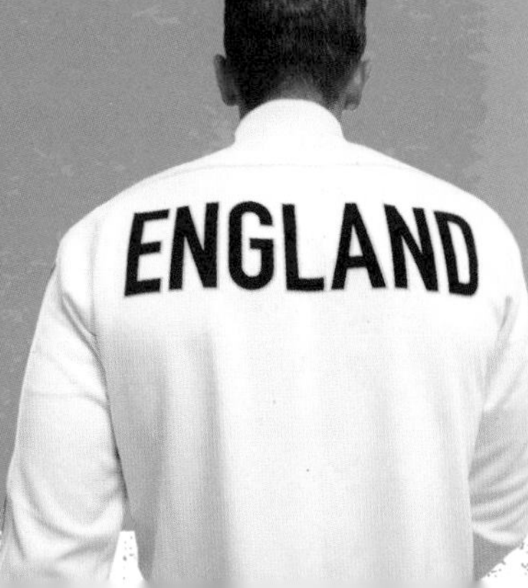
ENGLAND

HELLO, HARRY

Discover the incredible rise of the Tottenham and England super striker

HARRY KANE

Born: 28 July, 1993
Place of birth: London
Country: England
Club: Tottenham Hotspur
Previous clubs: Leicester, Norwich, Millwall, Leyton Orient (all loan)
Position: Striker
Preferred foot: Right
Boots: Nike

Harry Kane is a world-class goalscorer. With more than 200 career goals, stacks of Golden Boot awards and net-busting records, he's in a league with the planet's elite. The Tottenham and England legend has worked incredibly hard, rising from a teenager on loan in the lower leagues to become a fearsome forward and captain of his country.

Kane is lethal in Europe too. He's racked up Champions League records that rank him alongside heroes such as Messi, Ronaldo and Lewandowski. He's Tottenham's all-time top scorer in Europe and helped shoot the club to its first Champions League final. With Kane leading the line, Spurs will always be a danger!

Your awesome Football Idols guide to this goal great reveals all Kane's best bits, including amazing soccer stats and facts. From his first goals and trophies to becoming a Premier League superstar and leading his country on the world stage.

KID KANE

As a youngster, Harry was football crazy and worshipped the Spurs stars

Kane had footy fever from a young age. He enjoyed having a kickabout with his older brother, Charlie, and supporting England in tournaments. Aged six he joined Ridgeway Rovers, in north-east London. Harry impressed as a goalkeeper at first, but once he played outfield the coaches saw he had a natural scoring ability.

Having lived close to Tottenham's stadium, White Hart Lane, Harry became a big Spurs fan and often went to watch games. His favourite players were strikers such as Teddy Sheringham, Robbie Keane and Jermain Defoe – a trio that scored hundreds for the club.

"Most of my family are Spurs fans and I grew up 15 minutes from the ground, so I was always going to be a Spurs fan." Harry's family history made it almost impossible to become anything but a Tottenham player!

A young Kane would also spend hours watching clips of Ronaldo, the Brazilian striker, scoring and beating defenders. Seeing his heroes in action gave him the desire to one day do exactly the same!

FOLLOWING THE FOOTSTEPS

Long before he became a football idol, Kane was already walking a familiar path

David Beckham is nearly 20 years older than Harry Kane, but the pair still have a lot in common. They both played for the Ridgeway Rovers junior team and Beckham also had a spell with Tottenham when he was young, before joining Manchester United. Ridgeway are super-proud to have produced two legendary England captains!

As well as looking up to his Spurs heroes, Harry was also a fan of 'Becks'. He attended the David Beckham Academy and even met David at an event when he was 11. "David Beckham was a big role model of mine. He led by example on and off the pitch," Kane said shortly after being named as England skipper and he's definitely on his way to emulating his hero. Just like Beckham, Kane has become a huge player and dazzled in the Premier League, in Europe and on the international stage.

FOOTY FACT

Kane also went to the same school as David Beckham – Chingford Foundation School in London.

ACADEMY

Joining Tottenham's academy didn't come easily for Harry

Kane had highs and lows as a youngster trying to make his football future. From Ridgeway Rovers, he joined the Arsenal academy at the age of 9 – he could have gone pro for Spurs' fiercest rivals!

However, Arsenal released him after just one season, saying he didn't have the speed or physique needed. Harry returned to Ridgeway and worked hard to prove them wrong. He later spent a few weeks at Watford, and after impressing in a game against Tottenham, Spurs gave him a trial.

FOOTY FACT

Andros Townsend, Kane's future Tottenham Hotspur and England teammate, was also at Ridgeway Rovers.

ACTION

The 11-year-old Kane did enough to get a spot at their academy and his dream of becoming a Tottenham player could finally begin. His rejection by Arsenal at a young age gave him the motivation to succeed. Every time he scores against Arsenal, he remembers what happened – another reason why the Spurs fans admire him!

TEENAGE TOTTENHAM TALENT

The striker soon made a name for himself as a future Spurs star

Now part of his beloved Tottenham, Harry didn't want to disappoint during his teenage years. He preferred to play as a central striker, but if he needed to play wide, he did so to help his team. He did extra practice to develop his weaker left foot and heading ability.

As part of the Tottenham Under-16s, he scored at the renowned Chivas Cup and Bellinzona tournaments. Stepping up to the Under-18s, he blasted 18 goals in 22 games. The first team coaches couldn't ignore Kane's potential and when he was called up, he didn't look out of place.

Manager Harry Redknapp was keen to have Kane in his Premier League squad soon. Redknapp knew the teenager needed to keep scoring in youth games and on loan with a lower league club to give him experience of competitive football.

"I've scored goals in schools football, youth football, professional football, for Spurs, on loan. I've always wanted to score goals." No matter what level he played at, he was a top striker.

ENGLAND CALL

Playing his first youth game for his country was a massive moment

FOOTY FACT

Kane struck six goals in just 14 appearances for the England Under-19 team.

Shortly after first appearing on the Tottenham bench in October 2009, Kane got his first England call-up! He was included in the Under-17 squad alongside players like Ross Barkley and Conor Coady. The young Lions set off for the Algarve in Portugal, where Harry debuted against France.

Later that year, he helped England reach the Euro Under-17 finals. Sadly, illness ruled him out of the competition as England won the trophy. He was elated, but gutted to miss out on glory with his country!

His career with The Three Lions was up and running, and in 2010 he also helped the Under-19s reach their European Finals, set to take place in 2012.

LEYTON LOAN

Kane dropped down to League 1 to begin building up his football career

Kane felt his Tottenham bow was coming in the 2010-11 season, but the club sent him out on loan. He didn't arrive at a big club to take it easy – he joined Leyton Orient in League 1 and made his debut as a sub against Rochdale!

He started the next game and scored against Sheffield Wednesday, going on to net 5 goals in 18 games. The move was perfect for Kane – Orient was a club he knew well, having grown up not too far away. But it wasn't all good – he got his first red card at Huddersfield!

18

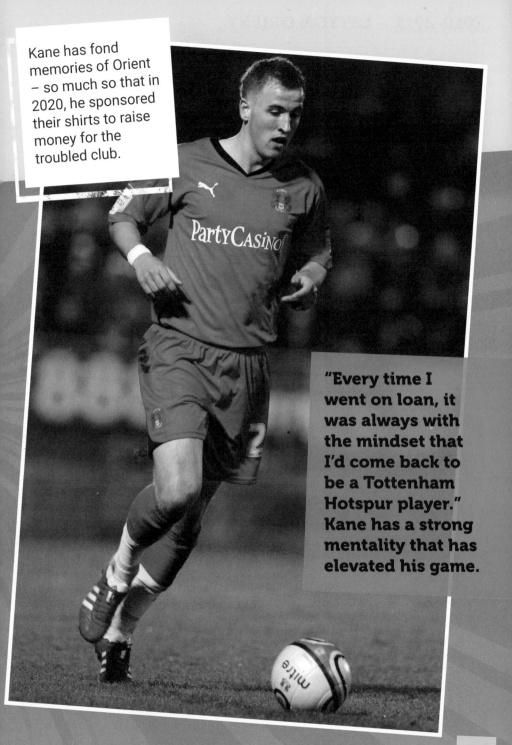

Kane has fond memories of Orient – so much so that in 2020, he sponsored their shirts to raise money for the troubled club.

"Every time I went on loan, it was always with the mindset that I'd come back to be a Tottenham Hotspur player." Kane has a strong mentality that has elevated his game.

SPURS START

Aged just 18, Kane got to pull on the Tottenham shirt to make his debut

Appearing for Orient was great, but Harry really wanted first-team action at Spurs. Shortly after turning 18, his dream came true and he made his Tottenham debut at home to Hearts in the Europa League in August 2011. His first six Spurs games all came in Europe!

On 15 December 2011, Harry struck his first Tottenham goal. It came in a Europa League game at Shamrock Rovers with a swivelled right-foot finish from close range.

A few weeks later, Kane made another loan switch to London neighbours Millwall in the Championship. He scored twice in his fourth game and went on to net 9 in 27 appearances. Harry impressed enough to be voted Millwall's Young Player of the Year, but had he done enough to kick-start his Spurs career?

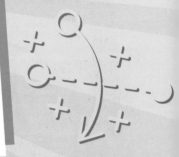

FOOTY FACT

Kane won a penalty during his Tottenham debut against Hearts, which he took himself, only to see the keeper save it!

PREMIER POSITION

After making his Premier League debut, Kane faced a testing time

The 2012-13 season was another that Kane will never forget – he played for three different clubs! There were highs and lows and moments that tested his confidence. He made his first Premier League appearance in Spurs' opening match, coming off the bench in a 2-1 loss at Newcastle.

He then made another loan move to Norwich in the Premier League, but broke his foot after two games. It kept him out for three months, but he made two more appearances at the end of 2012 before he was recalled. The striker didn't stay in London for long, though, as he moved on again, this time to help Leicester's promotion push from the Championship.

Harry scored twice for Leicester, but struggled to make the team and the Foxes remained in the Championship.

FOOTY FACT

At Leicester, Kane competed for a starting spot along with his future England teammate, Jamie Vardy.

WORLD STAGE

When he was 19, Kane took on the world's best young players at a FIFA finals

In the summer of 2013, Kane got his first taste of a FIFA World Cup finals at the Under-20 World Cup in Turkey. Kane's previous record of six goals for the England Under-19 team proved he could handle the international stage.

FOOTY FACT

Gareth Southgate was Kane's manager with the England Under-21 team. Southgate would later make Kane captain of the senior England team.

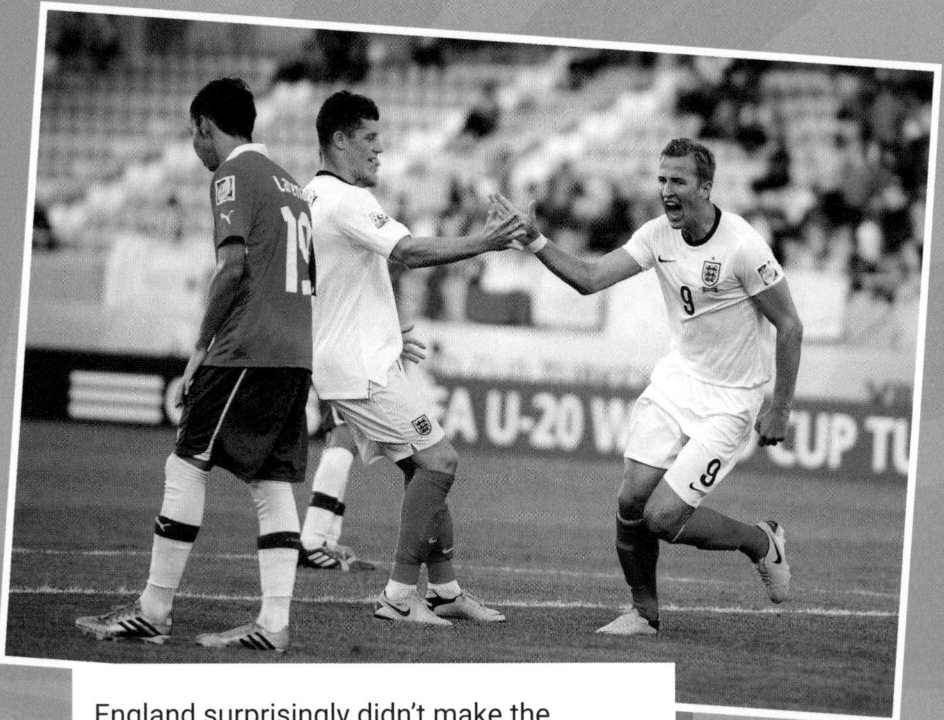

England surprisingly didn't make the knockout stage, but Kane scored against Chile in the group with a cool finish from the edge of the box. The 19-year-old took as much experience as possible from the tournament, hoping it would help him reach the senior squad.

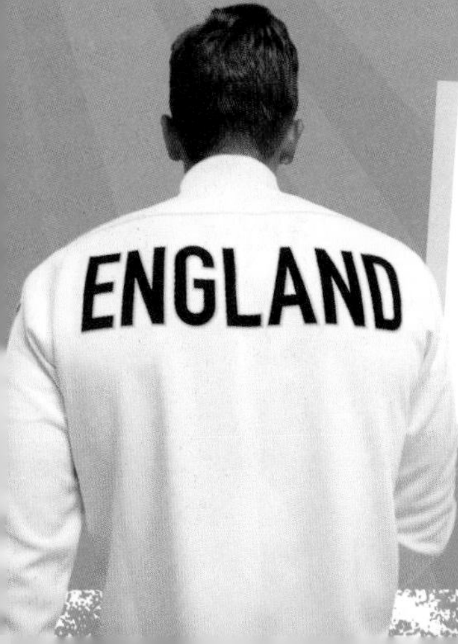
ENGLAND

In August 2013, he stepped up to the England Under-21s and came off the bench in a 6-0 win over Scotland. In his first Under-21 start, against San Marino, he blasted a hat-trick! His record at this age group was 7 goals in 14 games!

TOP FLIGHT STRIKE

Kane marked his first league start for Spurs with his opening Premier League goal

Harry had a long wait to get his first Premier League start for Tottenham, which came in April of the 2013-14 season. He bagged his first top-flight goal in a 5-1 win over Sunderland.

With his confidence sky-high after that goal, Kane kept his place in the team for the rest of the season. He netted in each of the next two games and fans were seeing their first signs of what an exciting talent the 20-year-old was. He easily outshone his international teammates Emmanuel Adebayor and Roberto Soldado!

The Tottenham manager at the time was Tim Sherwood. He was delighted with Kane's early displays. "He's a prolific goalscorer at the moment. He's a good finisher and I always knew he could step up," Sherwood said. Little did he know Kane would become one of the world's greatest strikers.

FOOTY FACT

The next time Kane played Sunderland in the Premier League, in September 2014, he unfortunately scored an own goal!

GOAL GLORY

The 2014-15 season was full of goals and glory for Kane!

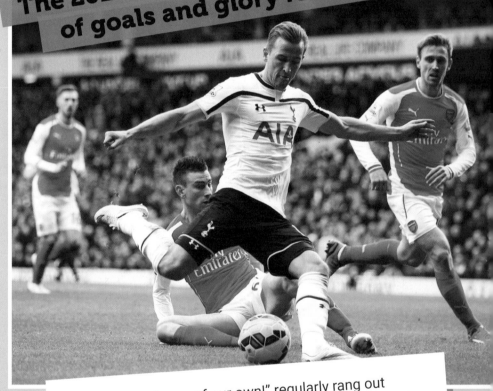

"Harry Kane, he's one of our own!" regularly rang out around White Hart Lane, as Harry's hot streak continued. He started the season with eight goals in eight cup games, including his first Spurs hat-trick, before his Premier League campaign took off after a late winner at Villa.

He finished with 21 goals in 34 games, matching the Premier League record of past Spurs stars Bale and Sheringham. In total he grabbed 31 from 51 appearances in all competitions.

Highlights included both goals in a 2-1 win over Arsenal – his first North London derby start – and another double in a 5-3 victory against Chelsea. He also picked up two Player of the Month prizes, was named PFA Young Player and made the official Premier League Team of the Year!

FOOTY FACT

The only real disappointment in Kane's 2014-15 season was when Spurs lost the League Cup final to Chelsea.

SAY WHAT?

Lots of football legends have praised Harry Kane's goal scoring powers

"Harry is second to none. As a striker, as a goalscorer, as a team player, as a leader, I think he is fantastic."

Jose Mourinho, Spurs manager, appreciates his star man. Everyone would want Kane in their team.

"He's always thinking about the goal in everything he does."

Zinedine Zidane, Real Madrid legend, knows that Kane is an instinctive goalscorer.

"He's the best goalscorer in the world. We have huge belief in him."

Gareth Southgate, England manager, knows that the country is in safe hands with captain Kane.

"Kane just doesn't care — he shoots from everywhere, he's like Cristiano Ronaldo."

Gary Lineker, former Spurs and England striker, suggests that he's got a wide range of goals up his sleeve.

"He is the complete centre-forward. I don't think there's anything that he can't do. He's got pretty much everything."

Alan Shearer, all-time leading Premier League goalscorer, realises Kane could someday outscore him. At the rate Kane's scoring at, we wouldn't be surprised.

WEMBLEY WONDER

Kane dazzled at Wembley when he played his first senior England game

With goals flowing at Tottenham, Harry fully deserved to be included in the England squad for the first time in March 2015. Manager Roy Hodgson was keen to use him as The Three Lions chased qualification for the Euro 2016 finals.

Kane debuted in the 72nd minute against Lithuania …
and scored a header 79 seconds later! "It's something
I've always dreamed of as a kid," Harry said afterwards.

Kane finished 2015 with eight appearances for his
country, including friendlies against tough teams like
France, Spain and Italy. He scored in two more Euro
2016 qualifiers, against Switzerland and San Marino.
Even with goalscorers like Wayne Rooney, Jamie
Vardy and Raheem Sterling as competition, his place
at the Euro 2016 finals was looking secure.

FOOTY FACT

**Kane's Lithuania strike was the third
fastest debut goal in England history.
The record is held by Spurs legend
Bill Nicholson, who scored after less
than 30 seconds of his debut in 1951.**

TOTTENHAM'S TOP 10

With Kane's club goal count racking up, he collected another famous number

"It's such an iconic number at Spurs," said Kane after being given the number 10 shirt. "When I was growing up, Keane and Sheringham were my idols and they wore 10, so it was always my dream to wear it." In just a few short seasons, Kane had proved to all of us that he deserved to wear it.

FOOTY FACT

Harry was the first Spurs striker to win the Premier League Golden Boot since Teddy Sheringham in 1993.

Harry didn't disappoint wearing the iconic number. He claimed his first Premier League Golden Boot with 25 goals. In total he netted 28 in all competitions, racking up his 50th senior club goal in just his 104th appearance.

Strangely, he didn't score for Tottenham in his first eight games in 2015-16, but then went on a scoring spree and also struck four for England in that campaign. He was in England's team at Euro 2016, where they lost to Iceland in the round of 16.

7 SLICK

Check out all the skills that make Kane such a quality striker

1 HEADING

He's one of the best in the business at scoring headers! His first England goal was a header, and 22 of his first 143 Premier League goals were from his noggin! He's a real danger from set pieces.

2 BOTH FEET

He's not scared to take a shot with his weaker foot. He's worked hard to make it accurate, scoring 32 Premier League goals with his left in his first nine seasons.

3 POWER

The hours Harry spends in the gym each week have paid off! He has the strength to hold the ball up, outmuscle defenders and use his power and pace to race clear.

4 PENALTIES

His ice-cool penalty technique has seen him score 20 penalties in the Premier League up to the end of the 2019-20 season, plus 9 for England.

SKILLS

5 LONG RANGE

Defenders can't give Kane space, even outside the box. He's scored epic efforts from distance against Chelsea, Arsenal and Wolves.

6 LEADERSHIP

The superstar leads by example and inspires teammates to match his effort. Harry's commitment and dedication make him a role model for younger squad members too.

7 SHOOTING EARLY

Catch the keeper by surprise! Kane knows that shooting early can catch the opposition off guard and lead to a goal – even if they aren't always the cleanest efforts.

OFF THE PITCH

Find out what his life is like when he's not banging in the goals!

SPORTS FAN

Harry's also a huge fan of American Football and watches the NFL in America on TV all the time. He's even been to NFL games at Wembley Stadium and at Tottenhham!

GOLF GUY

After training or during the summer break, Kane can often be seen on the golf course practising his swing and putting. He enjoys relaxing on the greens with his teammates!

ADVERT APPEARANCES

You've probably seen Harry appear in TV and social media adverts for big companies such as Nike, Coca-Cola and Beats headphones. He earns big money for it!

FOOTY FACT

Kane was awarded the special MBE award in December 2018 for his services to football. The awards are handed out by the British Royal Family!

SOCIAL STAR

Harry keeps the Spurs and England fans updated on what he's doing through his social media channels. He has ten million Instagram followers and three million Twitter fans, posting about his family, his teammates and how he's preparing for big games ahead.

LEAVING THE

Kane waved goodbye to White Hart Lane in 2017, a ground where he had scored so often

The 2016-17 season was an emotional time for Harry, his teammates and the Tottenham fans. It was their last at White Hart Lane, before they moved to a new super-stadium. Determined to give it a good send-off, Kane netted 29 Premier League goals to take another Golden Boot!

LANE

The striker also made his mark in the Champions League, scoring twice in the group stage. On New Year's Day 2017, Harry made his 100th Premier League appearance and scored a brace, taking his PL record to 59!

Spurs lost an FA Cup semi-final to Chelsea, a game Kane scored in. But he left White Hart Lane in epic style two weeks later, scoring in a 2-1 win over Manchester United, which secured second place. He then rounded off the season with seven goals in his last two matches!

CAPTAIN
KANE

One of Harry's highlights was becoming the England skipper for the first time!

Kane had already captained Tottenham, standing in for skipper Hugo Lloris at times, but in June 2017 he wore his country's armband for the first time in a massive World Cup qualifier against Scotland!

The 23-year-old didn't let The Three Lions down, grabbing his sixth goal in 18 international games during injury-time, which secured a 2-2 draw. The result against fierce rivals kept England on course to reach the World Cup.

Competing with Jordan Henderson for the honour, Kane's strong leadership and guaranteed starting place made him favourite for the role, though he wasn't named full-time England captain until a few weeks before the 2018 World Cup.

FOOTY FACT

The permanent England captain before Kane was Wayne Rooney. He stopped playing for England in 2017, but made one final international appearance in November 2018.

RECORD-BREAKING YEAR

In 2017, Kane became Europe's top striker ahead of Ronaldo and Messi!

Between January 1 and the end of December 2017, Kane netted 39 Premier League strikes in just 36 games, beating Alan Shearer's record of 36 goals in a calendar year – the first of many records that would fall that year. In total, Harry netted 56 goals in all competitions for club and country – two more than Messi and three more than Ronaldo in the same time period.

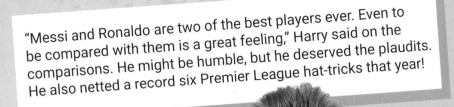

"Messi and Ronaldo are two of the best players ever. Even to be compared with them is a great feeling," Harry said on the comparisons. He might be humble, but he deserved the plaudits. He also netted a record six Premier League hat-tricks that year!

His 100th competitive goal for Tottenham arrived in September 2017, in a 3-0 Premier League win at Everton. He reached that total in only 169 games. In December, he also scooped his third Premier League Player of the Month award for the year!

FOOTY FACT

Kane was voted the England Player of the Year for 2017 by the England supporters.

HUNDRED HERO

Kane hit triple digits in the Premier League during a goal crazy 2017-18 season

Kane collected his 100th Premier League strike in a thrilling 2-2 draw at Liverpool in February 2018. He coolly slotted in a penalty in the 95th minute, though he'd missed from the spot earlier in the match!

FOOTY FACT

To celebrate Kane's 100th Premier League goal, he was given a special pair of Nike boots with '100' on them!

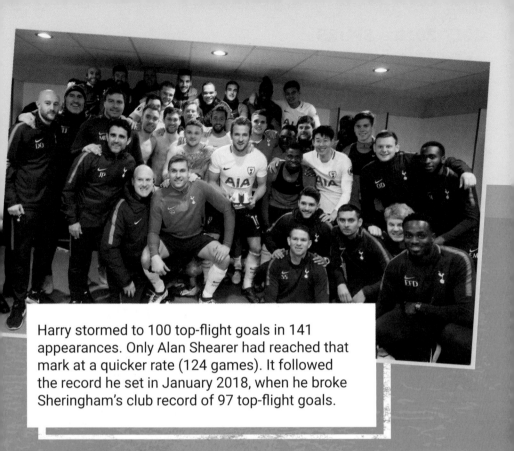

Harry stormed to 100 top-flight goals in 141 appearances. Only Alan Shearer had reached that mark at a quicker rate (124 games). It followed the record he set in January 2018, when he broke Sheringham's club record of 97 top-flight goals.

It wasn't just in the league where Kane was racking up the records. In February the striker also scored his ninth Champions League goal to become the first player ever to net nine in their first nine Champions League games. That ninth goal came in a dramatic 2-2 away match at Juventus' Allianz Stadium.

ROCKING IN RUSSIA!

The 2018 FIFA World Cup in Russia was a top tournament for England and Kane

England hadn't reached a World Cup semi-final since 1990 – before Harry was born! All that changed at the 2018 competition in Russia, when England stormed to the semis and Kane collected one of footy's most prestigious personal prizes.

England beat Tunisia 2-1 in the opening match, thanks to a double from captain Kane. He then hit a hat-trick in the 6-1 group stage win against Panama and scored again in the round-of-16 victory over Colombia. England then comfortably beat Sweden 2-0 to set up a semi-final with Belgium. Sadly they lost, but England had impressed on the world's biggest football stage!

Although The Three Lions didn't win a trophy, Kane did. He lifted the World Cup Golden Boot with his six strikes at the 2018 tournament. He finished with more goals than strike heroes like Griezmann, Ronaldo and the prodigious Mbappé.

GOAL-DEN GREAT

Check out all six of Harry's 2018 World Cup goals that gave him the Golden Boot

GOAL 1

Against Tunisia, Kane reacted quickly from just a few metres out as the goalkeeper pushed away a header. His smart right-foot volley sent the fans and team wild.

GOAL 2

In the 90th minute, Harry headed home with a clever finish to give England an essential 2-1 opening win over Tunisia!

GOAL 3

The first of Harry's hat-trick of goals against Panama was a fierce penalty high to the keeper's left in the 22nd minute.

GOAL 4

At the end of the first half, he struck another penalty that was almost identical to his first. That gave England an incredible 5-0 lead.

GOAL 5

A big slice of luck handed Kane his hat-trick against Panama. Ruben Loftus-Cheek's shot clipped his foot and looped into the net, leaving the keeper stranded!

GOAL 6

The striker's final World Cup goal was another perfect penalty. This time he sent the Colombia keeper the wrong way, as he drove the ball down the middle.

EURO ADVENTURE

Tottenham made their first appearance in a Champions League final

Unlike Arsenal, Chelsea, Liverpool and Man United, Tottenham had never appeared in a Champions League final. Kane and the gang changed that in 2018-19 when Spurs sealed a spot in club football's biggest game!

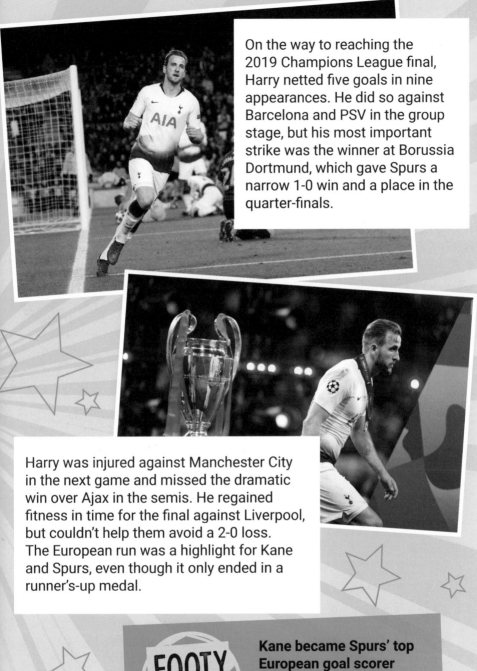

On the way to reaching the 2019 Champions League final, Harry netted five goals in nine appearances. He did so against Barcelona and PSV in the group stage, but his most important strike was the winner at Borussia Dortmund, which gave Spurs a narrow 1-0 win and a place in the quarter-finals.

Harry was injured against Manchester City in the next game and missed the dramatic win over Ajax in the semis. He regained fitness in time for the final against Liverpool, but couldn't help them avoid a 2-0 loss. The European run was a highlight for Kane and Spurs, even though it only ended in a runner's-up medal.

FOOTY FACT

Kane became Spurs' top European goal scorer in 2019. His winner at Dortmund was his 24th for the Londoners.

5 FUN

Take a look at some of the fun facts and weird records during Kane's fab footy career!

1 KEEPER KANE

Harry once played in goal for Spurs after keeper Hugo Lloris was sent off! Unfortunately he let in a goal, but he'd already scored a hat-trick in the 5-1 win against Asteras Tripolis.

2 AUGUST ANGUISH

Kane played over 14 games in five seasons before he scored a Premier League goal in August. He finally did so versus Fulham in August 2018!

FOOTY FACTS

3 OH, MY DAYS!

In July 2020, Kane became the first Premier League player to score in every month of the year and on every day of the week!

4 JUST FOUR YOU

Kane assisted all four of Son Heung-min's goals in a 5-2 Premier League win at Southampton in 2020. No player had done that before – he also scored the other goal!

5 HIT FOR SIX

He's the only Tottenham player ever to score 20 or more goals in a season for six seasons in a row. He's consistently a top-scorer!

ENGLAND ACE

He thrilled again for The Three Lions in 2019, setting records and topping goal charts!

Kane continued adding to his international goals in Euro 2020 qualifiers. He became the first England player to score in every match of a qualifying campaign, hitting 12 goals in eight games. He finished as top scorer in qualifying, ahead of Ronaldo, Lukaku and Gnabry.

He became the first to score consecutive hat-tricks for England. He netted three against Bulgaria in September and three against Montenegro in November. He scored 12 goals for his country in 2019, equalling the record for England goals in a calendar year.

Finally, he finished 2019 by banging in his 25th goal as England captain. Harry's displays for his country were world-class that year as he rose to sixth in the all-time England top scorer list, with 32 goals in just 47 games!

FOOTY FACT

In October 2019, Kane equalled the penalty record for England with his ninth spot kick success.

TOP 20

Going into 2020, he stormed to 20 Champions League goals!

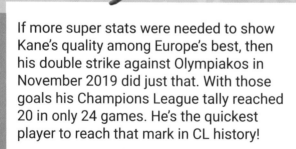

If more super stats were needed to show Kane's quality among Europe's best, then his double strike against Olympiakos in November 2019 did just that. With those goals his Champions League tally reached 20 in only 24 games. He's the quickest player to reach that mark in CL history!

That rate was way ahead of Messi, Ronaldo and Benzema. It also made Harry the fifth-highest English scorer in the Champions League, just 14 behind Wayne Rooney's record. At the start of the 2019-20 season, Kane also grabbed his first goals at the new Tottenham Hotspur Stadium.

Harry finished the season in July by clocking up his 200th club goal after netting against Newcastle. He needed just 350 appearances to reach it! By the end of the campaign his Tottenham record was an impressive 188 goals in all competitions, as well as the 16 he scored for his loan clubs as a teenager.

GREATEST GOALS

Look back at the best of the best from Kane's goal-packed career

BLUES BEATER

Opponent: Chelsea
Date: 10 January 2015

Harry skips past The Blues' midfield from out wide, then blasts a fierce drive across the keeper to send Spurs fans wild!

DERBY DELIGHT

Opponent: Arsenal
Date: 5 March 2016

In the North London derby, the striker took the ball from the touchline to spring a surprise curling shot beyond the Arsenal keeper.

BERLIN BELTER

Opponent: Germany
Date: 26 March 2016

Against the World Cup holders, Kane turned sharply in the box, made space and then drove low through a crowded goal area.

LETHAL LONG RANGER

Opponent: Everton
Date: 5 March 2017

Harry showed strength to win the ball with his back to goal, then turn past the Everton defence to shoot a rocket shot.

CHAMPION STRIKE

Opponent: Borussia Dortmund
Date: 13 September 2017

In the Champions League at Wembley, Kane powered down the left wing to blast an accurate left-foot finish into the net.

KANE CONTINUES

What next for the Spurs and England legend? Harry already has a goal record for club and country that matches the best. With 250 goals to his name, he can aim to become the Premier League's greatest, beating Shearer's 260 goals, and dream of having the all-time record for Spurs and England.

Personal prizes will always come his way. His trophy cabinet is stuffed with Golden Boots and Player of the Season awards, among others. He's determined to win big trophies at Spurs, having come close in several league campaigns and tournaments.

"I just want to win trophies. I don't think there's a day that goes past when I don't wake up and think I want to win." Watch this space — it's only a matter of time before he gets his hand on some major silverware.

There are not many strikers more dangerous than Harry. He loves hitting the back of the net and setting up his teammates in the hunt to win every game. Kane will carry on scoring for many years to come and put on a good show while he does!

BELGIUM
14 JULY 2018

CREDITS

Front Cover Sebastian Frej/MB Media Solutions/Alamy Images
Back Cover Michael Regan/PA Images/Alamy Images; Nick Potts/PA Images/Alamy Images
Graphics - Irina Qiwi/Shutterstock
6-7 Catherine Ivill/Staff – Getty Images Sport/Getty Images; Tottenham Hotspur FC/Getty Images.
8-9 – Pictures: AFP Contributor/AFP/ Getty Images. **Words:** Matt Barlow – dailymail.co.uk
10-11 – Pictures: Ross Kinnaird/Staff – Getty Images Sport Classic/Getty Images; Tottenham Hotspur FC/Getty Images; Brynn Lennon / Staff – Getty Images Sport/Getty Images. **Words:** Sam Cunningham – inews.co.uk
12-13 Craig Mercer/MB Media/Getty Images Sport/Getty Images; Pete Norton/Stringer – Getty Images Sport/Getty Images.
14-15 – Pictures: Matthew Ashton/Contributor – Corbis Sport/Getty Images; GLYN KIRK/Stringer – AFP/Getty Images. **Words:** Matt Barlow – Daily Mail
16-17 Julian Finney/Staff – Getty Images Sport/Getty Images
18-19 – Pictures: Dan Istitene/Staff – Getty Images Sport/Getty Images **Words:** James Maw – fourfourtwo.com
20-21 GLYN KIRK/Stringer – AFP/Getty Images; Julian Finney/Staff – Getty Images Sport/Getty Images.
22-23 Ross Kinnaird/Staff – Getty Images Sport Classic/Getty Images; Matthew Ashton/Contributor – Corbis Sport/Getty Images; Julian Finney/Staff – Getty Images Sport/Getty Images.
24-25 Chris Brunskill-FIFA/Getty Images; Jamie McDonald-FIFA/Getty Images.
26-27 – Pictures: ADRIAN DENNIS/Staff – AFP/Getty Images; AFP/Staff – AFP/Getty Images. **Words:** Dan Kilpatrick – espn.com.au
28-29 Paul Gilham/Staff – Getty Images Sport/Getty Images; Chris Brunskill/Staff – Getty Images Sport/Getty Images; Clive Rose/Staff – Getty Images Sport/Getty Images.
30-31- Pictures: Richard Heathcote/Staff – Getty Images Sport/Getty Images; PIERRE-PHILIPPE MARCOU/Contributor – AFP/Getty Images: Marc Atkins/Contributor – Getty Images Sport/Getty Images, Visionhaus/Getty Images Sport/Getty Images; Getty Images/Staff – Hulton Archive/Getty Images. **Words:** Sam McGuire – twenty3.sport, Darragh Murphy – joe.co.uk, Joe Shread – skysports.co.uk, Damien Lucas – hitc.com, goal.com.
32-33 Shaun Botterill/Staff – Getty Images Sport/Getty Images; Alex Livesey/Staff – Getty Images Sport/Getty Images.
34-35 GLYN KIRK/Stringer – AFP/Getty Images; Mark Leech/Offside/Getty Images. **Words:** Michael Cox – espn.co.uk
36-37 Clive Rose/Staff – Getty Images Sport/Getty Images.
38-39 Tottenham Hotspur FC/Getty Images; Paddy Power/Contributor – Getty Images Entertainment/Getty Images; NurPhoto - Contributor/NurPhoto/Getty Images; Clive Rose/Staff – Getty Images Sport/Getty Images.
40-41 – Pictures: Laurence Griffiths/Staff – Getty Images Sport/Getty Images; Tottenham Hotspur FC/Getty Images; Matthew Peters/Contributor – Manchester United/Getty Images.
42-43 Matthew Ashton – AMA/Contributor – Getty Images Sport/Getty Images; Mike Hewitt/Staff – Getty Images Sport/Getty Images; Shaun Botterill/Staff – Getty Images Sport/Getty Images.
44-45 – Pictures: OLI SCARFF/Contributor – AFP/Getty Images; Alex Morton/Stringer – Getty Images Sport/Getty Images. **Words:** Richard Martin – fr.reuters.com
46-47 GLYN KIRK/Contributor – AFP/Getty Images; Tottenham Hotspur FC/Getty Images; Simon Stacpoole/Offside/Getty Images.
48-49 ALEXANDER NEMENOV/Contributor – AFP/Getty Images; Catherine Ivill/Staff – Getty Images Sport/Getty Images; Quality Sport Images/Contributor – Getty Images Sport/Getty Images.
50-51 NICOLAS ASFOURI/Contributor – AFP/Getty Images; NICOLAS ASFOURI/Contributor – AFP/Getty Images; MARTIN BERNETTI/Contributor – AFP/Getty Images; JOHANNES EISELE/Contributor – AFP/Getty Images; JOHANNES EISELE/Contributor – AFP/Getty Images; JUAN MABROMATA/Contributor – AFP/Getty Images.
52-53 Maja Hitij/Staff – Bongarts/Getty Images; Craig Mercer/MB Media/Contributor – Getty Images Sport/Getty Images; Matthias Hangst/Staff – Getty Images Sport/Getty Images.
54-55 GLYN KIRK Stringer – AFP/Getty Images; Tottenham Hotspur FC/Getty Images, Catherine Ivill/Staff – Getty Images Sport/Getty Images; Pool/Getty Images Sport/Getty Images; DANIEL LEAL-OLIVAS/Contributor – AFP/Getty Images.
56-57 Chris Brunskill/Fantasista/Contributor – Getty Images Sport/Getty Images; Christopher Lee/Contributor – UEFA/Getty Images; Michael Regan/Staff – Getty Images Sport/Getty Images.
58-59 Rob Newell – CameraSport/Getty Images; Tottenham Hotspur FC/Getty Images; GLYN KIRK/Contributor – AFP/Getty Images.
60-61 Tottenham Hotspur FC/Getty Images; GLYN KIRK/Stringer – AFP/Getty Images; TOBIAS SCHWARZ/Staff – AFP/Getty Images; Rob Newell – CameraSport/Getty Images; Tottenham Hotspur FC/Getty Images.
62-63 Pictures: Alexander Hassenstein/Staff – Getty Images Sport/Getty Images. **Words:** James Benge – standard.co.uk